Helping Others
Avoid and Overcome
Pornography

OTHER BOOKS AND AUDIO BOOKS

BY G. SHELDON MARTIN

Be Still

10 Tips for Leaders, Spouses, and Parents
Helping Others
Avoid and Overcome
Pornography

G. Sheldon Martin

Covenant Communications, Inc.

Published by Covenant Communications, Inc.
American Fork, Utah

Printed in the United States of America
First Printing: April 2013

19 18 17 16 15 14 13   10 9 8 7 6 5 4 3 2 1

ISBN 978-1-62108-407-5

I wish to dedicate this book to those who have
had the faith and courage to turn to the Lord Jesus Christ
to overcome pornography.

Acknowledgments

I WISH TO ACKNOWLEDGE CHRISTY Hardman for her editorial and content contributions. I also wish to acknowledge Samantha Millburn and all of the wonderful Covenant Communications staff who made this project possible.

Contents

Introduction

I WORK AS A CLINICAL mental health counselor, and a mother once cornered me and, with trepidation in her voice, said, "My son has seen pornography. Is there any hope for him?"

I had a chance to visit with this young man, and he felt like he couldn't be a good priesthood holder, missionary, husband, or member of the Church because he had been exposed to pornography. His feelings had snowballed into hopelessness, low self-worth, and depression. In short, he felt he could never be a good enough man in the kingdom of God.

Of the many messages I hope individuals feel and believe as they read this book, the most important is this: nothing you have done has put you out of reach of the Redeemer of the world. To believe that you are lost and that you cannot be reclaimed by the Master is not only inaccurate, but it is also a lie shouted by the adversary.

I want to begin immediately with the message that there is hope. I have seen it. I have seen men and women break the bands of pornography. I have seen marriages rekindled, reformed, and recommitted. I have seen men and women turn from tears to joy.

Whoever you are, wherever you are, and whatever your experience has been with pornography, you can change. Whether this is your own struggle or the struggle of a family member, friend, or ward member, the Mighty One of Israel can make all things—even healing—possible.

Elder Holland has said, "To all of you who think you are lost or without hope, or who think you have done too much that was too wrong for too long, to every one of you who worry that you are stranded somewhere on the wintry plains of life and have wrecked your handcart in the process, this conference calls out Jehovah's unrelenting refrain, '[*My*] *hand is stretched out still.*'"[1]

This quote applies to those who struggle with the plague of pornography. It is common for you to feel you have done too much for too long. You have not. I beg you to return with new eyes and ears to the word of God. Learn of Him. Learn that His hand is stretched out still and will always be stretched out. And the Lord will not leave your loved ones comfortless. His hand is stretched out to all parties who have been affected. May we remember that the Lord's work and glory is to bring to pass *your* immortality and *your* eternal life (see Moses 1:39).

I have seen dozens of people change, and their change has less to do with techniques, education, or even desire, and more to do with their faith and hope in the Lord. I have found that those who change learn to rely on the Savior as their source of change. Of course, learning techniques, applying skills, and changing thought patterns is crucial in this battle, but never forget that relying on the Atonement of Jesus Christ is the most important factor.

I met with a man who perfectly illustrates this point. When we talked, he said he remembered the exact moment pornography took hold of him. He explained that he had seen pornography before, but that particular time was vivid and powerful. There was something about that moment that triggered a consumption of his time and energy. He went on to explain the battle that ensued over the next eight years. He had constant ups and downs. He felt depressed. He felt alone. He hurt his wife. However, that was not the end of his story.

After describing the torture, he told me about the changes he had made throughout the months and years. He asked, "Is it possible to feel as good as I do?" He told me he was home teaching again because he was not ashamed. He said he was playing with his children like he always wanted to do. He also stated, "I feel like the natural man is being rooted out of me." This individual took time out of his day to visualize the Savior, to ponder, and to pray to our Heavenly Father. He asked for specific help in his prayers for specific moments during the day. When he felt tempted, he thought about the Atonement and how the Lord could succor him because the Lord understands perfectly his temptation. He understood the doctrine that he had been granted an ability to choose. With this ability to choose, he made behavioral adjustments that involved filters and controlled use of electronic sources. He knew that changing his behavior was within his power only if he turned to the Lord for help. He had weekly discussions with his spouse about the victories he was experiencing. He and his wife began praying together for strength to improve their marriage. This man had the courage to check in often with priesthood leaders and loved ones who assisted in his change. This man processed over and over again the reasons he did not want to continue in pornography. He processed the hope that he could change, that what he really wanted was a loving relationship with his wife, and that he *wanted* to have a caring relationship. And he processed it over and over until it became a part of him.

This particular man used the Atonement and worked through challenges, and it has been multiple years since he has had any pornography problems. In fact, he has since told me, "I used to know the exact number of days since the last time I had viewed. Now, I can't even remember and rarely even think about it." This is a man who went from fearing he would fall every day to living with controlled confidence. This particular man went from knowing the facts about the Atonement of Jesus Christ to relying on its power for everyday strength.

Change is possible and important. As we discuss ways to do this, we must come to understand what we are fighting against. I wish to mention three introductory premises: pornography is addictive, the adversary is using pornography to attack Zion, and pornography can be overcome.

Pornography Is Addictive

As we begin, we need to understand that pornography is addictive. President Hinckley said, "It [pornography] easily becomes an addiction of the worst kind."[2]

Elder Oaks adds, "Pornography is also addictive. It impairs decision-making capacities and it 'hooks' its users, drawing them back obsessively for more and more."[3]

First, it is important to understand an addictive cycle. Most individuals have an emotional trigger that begins an obsessive thought process, which increasingly narrows until it seems that giving in and acting on the thought is the only option. The person *will* often give in, and afterward they feel regret and frustration, which in turn become emotional triggers that start the addictive cycle again. Pornography can become an addiction of the worst kind. More so than drugs, tobacco, or alcohol, pornography is extremely accessible, even for young children, and in most cases, it is less expensive, which makes it all the more dangerous. We cannot look the other way and pretend it doesn't exist or hope we and the people we love will automatically avoid it.

The Adversary Is Using Pornography to Attack Zion

We cannot ignore this plague because Nephi warns against such complacency: "For behold, at that day shall he [Satan] rage in the hearts of the children of men, and stir them up to anger against that which is good. And others will he pacify, and lull away into carnal security, that they will say: All is well in Zion; yea, Zion prospereth, all is well—and thus the devil cheateth their souls, and leadeth them away carefully down to hell" (2 Nephi 28:20–21).

We read of the early Saints who endured persecution, mobbing, and physical violence. Today, however, many Saints do not face such physical threats. But the adversary has not given up; he has just adjusted his plan. His tactics may appear more subtle, but his effects are every bit as damaging.

President Ezra Taft Benson taught, "The devil knows that if the elders of Israel should ever wake up, they could step forth and help preserve freedom and extend the gospel. Therefore the devil has concentrated, and to a large extent successfully, in *neutralizing* much of the priesthood. He has reduced them to *sleeping giants*."[4]

We must be aware of how Satan influences us. If we know what we are guarding against, we can be proactive in teaching correct principles as a defense. We can't afford to be "sleeping giants."

We need men and women who can stand for truth and fight against the evils of pornography. We need men and women who can defend the family and teach the beauties of a healthy sexual relationship between husband and wife. The days are past when members of the Church can unintentionally avoid pornography. It is time now for families to be proactive about teaching and discussing sacred sexuality.

Pornography Can Be Overcome

This book can serve as a source of hope. As I have previously stated, I have met with too many individuals who have already written themselves off. I have met with too many spouses who feel they can never have a trusting relationship again. I have met with too many individuals who feel the Lord's Atonement cannot reach them.

May I assert my personal conviction that through the Atonement of Jesus Christ, all things are possible! The Great Healer can heal "all manner of sickness" (Matthew 4:23). I know He lives. I know He loves us. I know that when turn to Him and His word, we can be healed.

I cannot stress enough that pornography can be overcome. In this book, I will suggest ten principles and ideas that can help you rely on the Atonement to overcome this plague. I hope these principles will serve as resources for parents, leaders, and spouses in their preemptive strike against pornography. Some of the best actions we can take in our homes are preventative. But may we never forget that if it is too late to prevent the onslaught of pornography, these tips will also lead you to the root of all positive change—the Atonement.

Learn to Deal with Sexual Thoughts in a Healthy Manner

INDIVIDUALS WILL OFTEN DESCRIBE THEIR method of overcoming inappropriate sexual thoughts as "I just tried to stop thinking about it." It's interesting that this is a common first reaction because that's really hard to do. Do not think about a yellow school bus. What did you think about? I am guessing school buses are traversing your frontal lobe as you read this.

There are two problems with the "just don't think about it" approach: first, the brain does not work that way; second, sexual thoughts are some of the most powerful thoughts a human being can have.

Our minds do not have a good ability to distinguish between "think about" and "don't think about." Both of these phrases actually increase the thought process. Many individuals who struggle with pornography try not to think about sexual thoughts by using sheer willpower. They try to absolutely, positively, for one last time, rid themselves of sexual thoughts. This white-knuckle approach usually lasts about three to six weeks. After time, it wears down their willpower, and they begin to feel hopeless and helpless.

Although the mind does not have a great ability to stop thinking, it does have an extremely powerful mechanism to change thought.

Stop thinking about a yellow school bus, and start thinking about a brown monkey. If we give the mind something to think about, it can turn its energy in a different direction.

It can do this because the mind is constantly making patterns. The process of undoing and recreating thought patterns does not happen by accident. In the instance of a negative thought we wish to be rid of, we must confront the thought by stating the *lie* and change it by stating the *truth*. Your goal is not to stop the intrusive thoughts—everybody has them. It is to *control what you do* in response to these thoughts and feelings.

The key ingredient to forming a new pattern is consistency. You will not accidently be able to control your thoughts, especially if a pattern of inappropriate thoughts already exists. If you want to be successful in overcoming an inappropriate thought, you have to spend time controlling that thought, which means you need to practice. Consistency is the key ingredient to changing thought. It will not happen without practice.

I always teach my clients the three *C*s in the process of changing a thought: *confront*, *challenge*, and *change*.

Confronting a thought is acknowledging that the thought exists. Pretending that you are not attracted to or tempted by pornography is not a helpful or healthy step. Confronting a thought gives yourself permission to evaluate and decide what you will do with that thought.

To challenge a thought, identify the incorrect nature of the rationalization or justification you might use to entertain a thought.

The third step is to then change the thought. Because we have power to adjust our thoughts, we can send our brain an appropriate message. This process cannot be done only one time. In fact, the phrase "by small and simple things are great things brought to pass" (Alma 37:6) is very applicable to changing thought patterns. You must do it over and over again until the new, appropriate thought takes root.

Let me illustrate these steps with an example. John goes to work and begins to feel overwhelmed with sexual thoughts. An attractive coworker walks by, and John's mind begins to process inappropriate sexual thoughts. Suddenly, he has a desire to search for pornography on the Internet at work. John *confronts* the thought by thinking, *I am feeling sexually inclined because that woman is attractive. I am tempted to look at pornography because I am entertaining inappropriate thoughts.* John can then *challenge* his thoughts by thinking, *If I entertain these thoughts, they will lead to viewing pornography, masturbating, feeling depressed, isolating my family, acting grumpy at home, disappointing my wife, and regretting this decision. I know that pornography and inappropriate relationships do not fit on the road I am headed down. Think of what either of these actions would do to my career, family, Church standing, and ultimately my standing before the Lord.*

John can finally *change* his thought by thinking, *The Lord has given us His crowning creation of women. They are beautiful and wonderful. The Lord wants us to have healthy sexual relationships, and the healthiest relationship occurs between a man and a woman who are eternally married. Honoring my covenants will lead to a happiness that is infinitely greater than the temporary pleasure entertaining inappropriate sexual thoughts can bring. I choose to be a good father and husband. Entertaining inappropriate sexual thoughts does not fit with where I am going.*

This example demonstrates the process of confronting, challenging, and changing a thought. I reemphasize that this process takes practice. It will not happen by accident, and the more you practice this process, the more automatic it will become.

When the Savior began His ministry, He fasted for forty days. At the end of Christ's fast, Satan came tempting Him. I imagine that the Lord was hungry. He had a mortal tabernacle, and He must have felt hunger like you and I feel hunger. In Matthew, we read about Satan's temptations and the Savior's responses.

Like all stories of the Master, the list of lessons learned grows larger the more we study. But one lesson we can identify is how the Savior dealt with a physical urge. Matthew 4:3–4 reads, "And when the tempter came to him, he said, If thou be the Son of God, command that these stones be made bread. But he answered and said, 'It is written, Man shall not live by bread alone, but by every word that proceedeth out of the mouth of God.'"

Notice particularly what the Lord says and does not say. The Lord does not try to fight Satan's temptation by claiming He is not hungry or that He does not like food; instead, He deals with this temptation by stating a higher, nobler reason for not wanting to eat: He states that man cannot live by bread alone. I believe the Savior is pointing out that His mission is far above gratifying physical desires.

Think of how this simple example applies to those trying to overcome inappropriate sexual thoughts. If individuals try to fight against sexual temptation by telling themselves they do not desire sexual relations or that sexual relations are never appropriate, they are going to constantly feel disconnected because no matter how much they try to cognitively tell themselves they do not have sexual urges, the body reminds them that they do. Contradicting those natural feelings by trying to convince themselves cognitively that those feelings are not real or important will eventually lead to them feeling overwhelmed, stressed, and worn out.

If they can approach these thoughts like the Savior did, they will be more successful. The Savior had a much more powerful reason to abstain. He knew that "man cannot live by bread alone" and that by partaking in the moment, He would forfeit longer-lasting blessings in the future. Likewise, we must spend time developing reasons to choose to remain free from pornography.

President Hinckley taught this same framework about pornography when he said, "When tempted, we can *substitute* for thoughts of evil thoughts of Him and His teachings."[5] Notice the word President Hinckley used: *substitute*. There must be an acknowledgment of current thoughts and an active process of "substituting" new thoughts.

I have had clients who take this framework too lightly. These new thoughts must be deep and powerful, or they will not work because sexual thoughts are so powerful. If the thoughts are not powerful, then rationalization will quickly creep in.

For example, I worked with a man who wanted to overcome his addiction to pornography. His initial thought was, "So I do not get divorced someday." This thought may be powerful for some, but this man was not yet married, so in the moment of temptation, he would quickly rationalize that he would be sure to fix this problem before marriage.

His reason was not deep and powerful, and soon it became necessary to push himself to find a reason real enough for him in the moment. He began thinking about the positive effect he could have currently as a righteous priesthood holder. He processed the thought that he had made covenants. He processed the thought that this was not a "someday" issue but that he had to choose to remain free from pornography today to build God's kingdom. For him, these reasons were more important and more powerful.

I love hearing powerful statements that individuals have developed. The thoughts are different, but there is a common theme in truly effective thoughts. Powerful, effective motives include the Atonement, the family, and the person's long-term life.

I have seen individuals post letters from their children at work. These letters will often express the child's love for their parent. I have seen individuals place family pictures as the background screen for their computer. I have heard of individuals who post encouraging scriptures on their mirror in the bathroom. These individuals have all formed powerful reasons and have used physical reminders of why they are changing.

To further illustrate this principle, think about fasting as an example of how motivation so often determines a true fast. Think of how easily we can rationalize eating during a fast if we are not fasting for a reason. Maybe you have experienced thoughts like, "I have been feeling sick. I should probably fast next week"; "It's still before midnight. I'll eat now and fast longer tomorrow"; or "I have not yet started with a prayer. I'll eat and then start right."

Contrast these examples with times when an individual is fasting for a loved one who is sick or for a needed blessing for the family. Our reason overcomes rationalization. When the thought of hunger hits, we quickly replace it with reasons to continue to fast. Likewise, individuals must process the reasons they are going to give up pornography.

There are some important elements in developing powerful replacement thoughts. First, write down reasons why you want to give up pornography. These thoughts need to be powerful. Include thoughts of family, future family, and the Savior and His teachings.

Second, find multiple times during the day to practice confronting, challenging, and changing your thoughts. You know the times, places, and experiences when you are most tempted. Practice visualizing and changing your thought process at those times.

Instead of spending energy trying to white-knuckle your way through not thinking about pornography, spend the energy being proactive: confront, challenge, and change your thought process.

Third, practice this process many times. This can be done through journaling, self-talk, visualization, and modeling. But more important than the method is the *frequency*.

Individuals who struggle to change the way they think often do not practice, visualize, or journal enough. If you only think about changing a thought process after you have had a setback, when you are speaking with a parent or bishop, or during general conference, you are not practicing enough to change a thought process. I encourage individuals to practice this process five to ten times a day. Practice out loud while driving to work. Practice by visualizing a better action during a temptation. Practice by writing in a journal about the reasons you are changing your thoughts. Frequency is the key.

Please know that this process works. I will often share with individuals struggling with pornography that those who do not struggle with pornography do not spend the emotional energy trying to change the thought process—it is already built in. Often, they will have a difficult time believing that it is possible to not spend so much emotional energy.

To help them understand, I ask them to describe feelings involved in another bad habit in which they do not struggle—drinking alcohol, for example.

"How much do you think about not drinking alcohol?" I ask.

Usually, they tell me they spend very little time, if any, thinking about alcohol. I often push them further and ask, "You mean every time you walk into a convenience store, you do not contemplate and evaluate whether or not you should buy a beer?"

At about this time, they begin to realize they already have ingrained reasons for why they do not want to buy a beer at a convenience store. I tell them I have other clients who struggle with alcohol consumption, and for them, going to the store is a battle every time. They then see that it is possible to be around a trigger without allowing it to govern their thought process.

Changing a thought process means it will often become harder before it becomes easier. It's natural to resist change, but as we confront, challenge, and change our thoughts, we can form new automatic patterns and begin to think differently.

The goal is to process thoughts in a healthy manner. This does not mean we will rid ourselves of sexual thoughts—it means we must learn to control them. Remember, we are agents to act and not be acted upon (see 2 Nephi 2:14).

Practical Applications

Spouses—Be open to helping your spouse reconstruct or change their thoughts. A spouse (or parent) can express out loud the incorrect nature of some thoughts and the correct nature of another, higher cause. The statements you come up with must be powerful, and they may take time to develop. Do not be offended if the reason *you* feel they should give up pornography is not *their* reason. Someone's reasons will change over time. If you feel your spouse's reason should be for their children but losing their job is more powerful to them, then allow them to start with their reason. Change is most effective when they feel internally motivated, when giving up pornography is their decision.

When can you and your spouse sit down
to discuss thought patterns?

_____

_____

Parents—Teach children to pray for specific help with the thoughts and times of day they struggle with. We know Heavenly Father can help us change our very nature. He can help us change the way we think. Ask for His help. Too many individuals obliquely approach this challenge and apply the power of prayer much too generally in their lives. I love when I hear of individuals who pray for strength for a very specific situation. We know when and how we are tempted. Pray for specific help before and during times of temptation, and thank Heavenly Father afterward. The more you involve the Lord with this process, the more you will feel His influence and recognize His tender mercies, and it can be a very sweet experience.

Leaders—Understand that overcoming pornography is more than just willpower. It is a reconstructing of thought. This process often takes someone else to help flesh out the thoughts. It is often helpful to those struggling to say these thoughts out loud. Finding someone else to help with this process can be extremely beneficial.

In a handbook training, Elder Quentin L. Cook said, "With the consent of a member struggling with pornography, an experienced high priest could receive an assignment from the bishop to provide the extensive counseling and coordinate other assistance that the member may need."[6]

Who is a mature high priest who can work with this
individual? (Ensure that both you and the member
feel comfortable with this choice.)

_____

_____

_____

Tip #2
Teach and Understand Sacred Sexuality

TOO OFTEN INDIVIDUALS APPROACH SEXUAL relations with the attitude that "sex is dirty, nasty, and inappropriate, but save it for the one you love." This message, although often not stated so directly, is portrayed in our cultural community. Sexual intimacy is beautiful and fulfilling. It is the highest form of bonding that two human beings can experience, but when two individuals attempt to engage in the highest form of human bonding with no legal, lawful, eternal, social, familial, relational, or covenantal relationship, the result is a feeling of emptiness and loneliness. It is an object lesson of total unity between husband and wife. The Lord intended that a man and woman be united in every way, including sexually.

The "For the Strength of Youth" pamphlet states, "Physical intimacy between husband and wife is beautiful and sacred. It is ordained of God for the creation of children and for the expression of love between husband and wife." In my experience, children often get the "birds and the bees" talk and understand that one of the reasons for sexual intimacy is the creation of children. However, many parents with whom I counsel rarely, if ever, talk to their children about the fact that sexual intimacy is also for the expression of love.

I know parents can feel uncomfortable talking about the wonders of sexual relations with their children. But they are going to learn it somewhere; should it not be from us? When humans reach puberty, they begin to feel a connection to individuals of the opposite sex. At first they may be confused, but over time, they accept that boys or girls are cute. We do not need to teach children that feeling attracted to the opposite sex is a bad thing because it's not. In fact, I see this as a real tender mercy from the Lord. Someone once asked me, "Why doesn't the Lord keep us from feeling that way until we are married?" We already have a challenge with too many young people not seeking a companion to get married. We don't want to compound that by taking away any feelings they may have for each other. These feelings help instruct us and draw us near one another.

What is sacred sexuality? Elder Holland said,

May I stress that human intimacy is reserved for a married couple because it is the ultimate symbol of total union, a totality and a union ordained and defined by God. From the Garden of Eden onward, marriage was intended to mean the complete merger of a man and woman—their hearts, hopes, lives, love, family, future, everything. Adam said of Eve that she was bone of his bones and flesh of his flesh, and that they were to be "one flesh" [Genesis 2:24] in their life together. This is a union of such completeness that we use the word *seal* to convey its eternal promise. The Prophet Joseph Smith once said we perhaps could render such a sacred bond as being "welded" to one to another.

But such a total union, such an unyielding commitment between a man and a woman, can only come with the proximity and permanence afforded in a marriage covenant, with solemn promises and the pledge of all they possess—their very hearts and minds, all of their days and all their dreams.

Can you see the moral schizophrenia that comes from *pretending* you are one, pretending you have made solemn promises before God, sharing the physical symbols and physical intimacy of your counterfeit union but then fleeing, retreating, severing all such other aspects of what was meant to be a total *obligation*?[7]

Elder Holland teaches so clearly the concept of union—total union. He says to teach children that sexual relations are bonding and unifying and meant to be enjoyed; however, Satan tries to convince us that there is a shortcut to total unity, that what we ultimately want is a small, intense experience; however, whether recognized or not, we truly seek total union.

It is important to teach the difference between intimacy and sex. Intimacy involves a total, committed relationship, whereas sex can involve two individuals who may or may not be committed to one another.

To illustrate this point, I often use an analogy with my clients. I ask them to imagine a fully assembled roof lying in the middle of the street. I ask them to describe the first words that come to mind. They will often describe the awkward nature of a roof without a house. It seems out of place and doesn't serve a purpose. I will ask follow-up questions like, "Aren't roofs useful? Do they not serve an important, even crucial, purpose?" Of course, they answer in the affirmative but explain that a roof without a house is not serving its purpose.

I ask them to describe when the roof serves its purpose, and they say it is when it is placed on top of a home. When there are walls, floors, windows, doors, paint, carpet, etc. The roof fulfills its role because it completes a home. Then I explain the parallel. Sexual intimacy alone is like the roof in the street. It will never fulfill its purpose without union. We need to teach that sexual intimacy is the highest form of union and it completes a relationship; it does not define it.

I hesitate to be so bold, but I believe that two human beings who love each other, serve each other, are sealed to each other, raise children together, attend parent teacher conference together, etc., can be more bonded and more united in sexual experiences than anyone else. I believe two Latter-day Saints who love and respect each other have the strongest intimate moments. I think it is important that we teach that what we really want in a sexual relationship can be fully realized only through the great plan of happiness. Sex is not bad; it is sacred.

To help understand that sex is not dirty and nasty, it is helpful to review what we know about the eternal nature of the powers of procreation. We know little about the distinguishing features among telestial, terrestrial, and celestial beings. The revelations are clear, however, that one distinguishing feature that celestial couples possess that no one else will possess is the sacred power of procreation. Sex is not dirty, nasty, and yucky. It is beautiful and glorious and celestial.

Sometimes families feel hesitant to discuss these topics, and they want to defer to someone else. The family is the best place to learn these concepts. Parents know what type of environment their children live in. They understand the culture where they live. There is not one worldwide application of when and how to teach children these principles because the world is different from place to place; therefore, it is important for parents to teach according to their family's needs and circumstances.

I served my mission in Paris, France. When I was there, the advertising and acceptance of sexuality was much different from where I grew up in Los Angeles County, and my hometown was much more open than the town I live in now. The messages are everywhere. Please do not hesitate to have open discussions with your children about this topic. If we do not talk, we run the risk of having them exposed to only inappropriate media messages about what sex is.

There is not one standard about when and what to cover, but I think we can be fairly confident that if children have already gone or are going through puberty, they are thinking about these subjects. I am often asked about the danger of planting seeds of inappropriate behavior by asking about sex, and this is a legitimate concern. I would use the "For the Strength of Youth" pamphlet as a standard to read together and then ask your children if they have questions about that. The Spirit will let you know what to say and how to say it.

It is important to have a loving and open relationship when discussing this topic. Remember that *how* you discuss intimacy is as important as *what* you discuss. It is healthy for parents and children to have these talks, and it is healthy for husbands and wives to have these talks.

For some individuals, talking about sex is extremely foreign and feels awkward. It could be that couples who cannot discuss sex experience frustration when they try to have sexual experiences. It is okay for a couple to discuss their feelings about their intimate relationship. It is okay to discuss frequency, to talk about what is attractive and what is not. It is okay to discuss these subjects and more. But above all, *have* the discussions.

Practical Applications

Spouses—Seek to help each other gain trust. Seek to bond in every way. Go on dates, hold hands, kiss, make dinner together, and attend the kids' events together. Believe that you can rebuild bonding.

Parents—The home is the best venue to teach this sacred truth. Teach about the sacredness of sexuality. You can use a family home evening, personal interviews, late-night discussions, etc. Decide together when you feel it would be a good time to discuss this topic with your children and what you will discuss.

Leaders—Help those you preside over to understand the sacred nature of intimacy. Help them understand that what they truly want, pornography cannot provide. You may feel impressed to hold a separate meeting or to discuss this in private interviews. Help the youth understand the sacred nature of sexuality.

How do you feel you could best impress
this topic upon those you serve?

_____

_____

_____

If Necessary, Seek Counsel from Caring Professionals

ONE OF THE MOST COMMON questions I am asked regarding those involved in pornography is, "How do I know if someone needs professional counseling?"

I have also met with some who feel there is never a time to turn to a professional counselor. President Hinckley clearly taught, "Have the courage to seek the loving guidance of your bishop and, if necessary, the counsel of caring professionals."[8] President Hinckley and other prophets have been clear that there is a time for professional counseling. He did, however, use the term *if necessary*, so there is also a time when professional counseling is not needed.

As a general rule, I often say that if people are displaying evidence of addictive behavior, counseling may be useful in helping them overcome pornography.

How do you know if you or a loved one is addicted to pornography? Evaluate the level of addictive behavior by analyzing the following: tolerance, withdrawal, increase in amounts, unsuccessful efforts to cut down, excessive time spent to obtain pornography, neglect of important social, occupational, or recreational activities, and continuation of usage even with a clear understanding of the problem.[9]

Tolerance is an indication of addictive behavior because it is an increase of amount with diminished effects. Often individuals who have developed a tolerance to pornography can look at pornography for longer periods of time with decreased amounts of pleasure. Many times, an individual can look at pornography for thirty minutes to an hour before they are even aroused. An individual can still have a very serious problem even if arousal comes quickly, but tolerance is an indicator of addictive behavior.

Like any addictive behavior, going off pornography can bring signs of withdrawal. Withdrawal means that cessation will bring distress. An individual who is addicted to pornography may become very irritable if they are unable to access it. This impairment may cause distress in the workplace, at home, or even in social settings. For example, if the family is going on vacation where there is not Internet access, this may cause distress, irritability, and even impairment to the individual.

If someone begins to take in larger amounts than intended, this can be a red flag to a serious problem. It is important to recognize that in most cases, the addict or user wants to stop viewing pornography; therefore, if someone begins to spend more and more time, this indicates an addiction.

In schools, teachers and authority figures often teach kids about gateway drugs—meaning that when someone begins one drug, over time the usage of the drug changes. This concept also applies to an individual who is addicted to pornography.

Someone with addictive behavior does not remain content with one form, so over time the source will change. In the example of pornography, individuals may begin with viewing still pictures, then start calling sexual-content phone numbers, then move to interactive sexual chat rooms, then movies, etc. If the source is changing, these individuals are displaying addictive behavior.

If individuals have had unsuccessful efforts to cut down, it is an indicator that this behavior is becoming addictive. This may seem simple, but if individuals have tried to stop multiple times and can't, there is a definite problem. The old adage applies, "If you do what you have always done, then you will get what you have always gotten." If they have tried to stop multiple times and have been unsuccessful, the chain needs to be scrambled, and something needs to be different this time.

Often those who are addicted will spend a great deal of time and effort to obtain pornography. The efforts might include breaking through multiple filters, volunteering to stay home, faking sick to get time alone, and staying late at work. They might maneuver around the house to try to get time alone for hours or identify ways to use the Internet without a spouse or parent knowing or research data plans on smart phones to avoid spikes in charges from viewing pornography.

A major red flag is when individuals give up important social, occupational, recreational, or even religious activities to obtain the substance. Pay attention to activities that seem to drop off quickly. Clients have told me that when they are viewing pornography, they stop going to the gym, stop home teaching, stop being diligent at work, do not want to golf with their friends, etc. This behavior does not mean that the next time a family member stays home from church, they are addicted to pornography. Don't fill in blanks that may not exist, but be aware that this is a typical behavior of those who are addicted.

The last and one of the clearest indicators of addictive behavior is that individuals continue use even though they know it is a problem and will continue to be. It breaks my heart to meet with clients who know that if they continue to view pornography, their marriage, family, career, standing in the Church, and social relationships will suffer. The whirlpool of sin has no mercy, no matter how desperately a person wants to get out.

You do not need professional training or have to have a degree to begin to evaluate if someone needs professional help. I developed some questions that might help evaluate addictive behaviors. There is no rule set in stone, but these questions might help you get a feel for the level of seriousness.

- At what age did you begin looking at pornography? (Addictions have history, so even if the person has repented, it is helpful to know the whole history.)
- When you began viewing pornography, how often would you look at it? (There is no strict number to look for, but a fifteen-year-old who has viewed pornography once is completely different from a thirty-year-old viewing three times a week.)
- When you began viewing pornography, for how long would you view each time? (Look for levels of tolerance here. Some individuals who are addicted can view pornography for longer periods of time with diminished pleasure. I have had clients who can view pornography for hours with little effect on them.)
- How many times a week do you currently view pornography, and for how long?
- How many times have you attempted to stop viewing pornography? (It's very important to understand that addictions control much of a person's life. You are looking for evidence that your loved one knows this habit is harming them and they do not have the ability to stop.)

- To how many bishops have you confessed? Or, how many times have you spoken with your parents? (This will help with history. Some have confessed to dozens of bishops.)
- How has pornography affected your performance at work? (A big indicator is poor work performance because a person is spending time searching pornography on the Internet.)
- How have the types of pornography use changed (e.g., R-rated, X-rated, phone calls, pictures of pornography, video, interactive, etc.)?
- What efforts do you make to view pornography (e.g., volunteering to stay home, staying late at work, extended lunch breaks, isolation in a bedroom)?

These questions can help you understand the level of seriousness of addictive behavior. As you discuss these questions with a loved one, it is important to do it with love. If someone feels interrogated, that feeling could cloud their desire to change. Explain to them that these questions will help you help them better.

Even when you identify an addictive behavior, you may wonder if you need a counselor. Professional counselors are not ecclesiastical leaders and should never attempt to cross that line. Professional counselors are not to take the role of a bishop or a parent. However, a counselor can offer some helpful tools to sustain and support a family and bishop in this process.

One of the first benefits a counselor can provide is a listening ear. Sometimes individuals dealing with a pornography problem need to express the frustration they are feeling with themselves and the situation. Counselors can offer an encouraging word when there are setbacks. Addictive behavior often changes in stages. Most often, but not always, change happens with multiple ups and downs but hopefully with an upward slope. When an individual does have a setback, they face a crossroads of giving up and continuing down the path of sin or applying the Atonement and continuing to try. Counselors can be wonderful coaches and cheerleaders to encourage struggling individuals to keep trying.

Remember, cognitive restructuring takes time, effort, and dedication. Most professional therapists are trained in at least basic cognitive behavioral techniques. A professional therapist can train and teach an individual how to change inappropriate thoughts as a skill and help you or your loved one practice and then follow up and report back.

There are other skills besides cognitive restructuring that a therapist can help with. Therapists might be able to help identify when and how the incidents occur. They can work with an individual to identify times, places, and situations of the occurrences.

Therapists can also be great with follow-up. A client can sign a release of information that will allow a therapist and bishop to communicate. Working with a therapist as a resource can help bishops, parents, and spouses work as a team instead of feeling isolated in the problem.

One of the clearest indicators of successful treatment is rapport between therapist and client. It is important that clients feel comfortable with their therapists. Therapy can bring a healthy placebo effect. When people acknowledge that they have a problem and resolve to meet with a therapist, their committed attitude can be the added measure of motivation.

Each case is different, but it may be beneficial to use a complete approach when dealing with pornography issues. This means it may be necessary to have individual, couple, and group counseling. Individual counseling can help an individual build the skills they need. Couple counseling can focus on strengthening and rebuilding your marriage or other committed relationship, and group counseling, such as the twelve-step program, can help increase hope and offer peer support so the client doesn't feel alone.

When looking for a professional counselor, find one that has a moral belief that pornography is wrong. If a counselor does not believe pornography is a problem, they may challenge the idea of wanting to change or use inappropriate techniques.

For example, a counselor might try to use a flooding technique, encouraging clients to look at pornography until they "get sick of it." We know doctrinally that some techniques like this are not appropriate and will not work.

Possibly above all else, ensure that a counselor is compassionate and kind. Breaking addictive cycles is an uphill struggle, and it is important to have a supportive, caring individual who will help when times are tough.

It is important to recognize that some individuals do just fine without a counselor. This chapter is not intended to state that all need counseling. However, if the problem has developed into a strong addiction, individuals should seriously consider using every resource possible, including a good, caring counselor.

Practical Applications

Spouses—If you feel that your spouse needs professional counseling, ensure that the time is right. Counseling has a negative connotation for some people. Your spouse needs to acknowledge that there is a problem, an action which can be difficult and humbling. Be sensitive about how and when you suggest professional counseling, and make sure you are both calm when you bring it up. If you bring it up as a threat or jab, it will not likely be received well. For example, if a spouse yells, "Maybe it is time for you to see someone to fix your porn problem!" the odds of that person feeling encouraged to change decreases greatly.

Parents—If you feel that your son or daughter needs professional counseling, do research to find the right type of counselor, one you and your child feel comfortable with. If you find a counselor you love but your child does not, you may want to keep trying. Also, parents, please ensure that your child is demonstrating signs of an addiction. Too many times, I have met with a child who has viewed pornography one time by accident, and the parents have set up an appointment with me, the bishop, a psychiatrist, and the stake president. Slow down and be loving! We live in a world where these types of images are all around us. As time goes on, the percentage of individuals who inadvertently come across pornography is rising. Even if children initially seek after pornography, they probably don't need professional counseling at that point, but they will need full confidence, trust, and love from a parent.

Leaders—Do research to find a list of six or seven counselors to whom you can refer to ensure that your member and the counselor have good rapport. If you have members who are attending LDS twelve-step programs, strongly encourage them to attend with sponsors. Individuals who attend with sponsors are much more successful. This may be another place to use those mature high priests in your ward; perhaps a former bishop who is retired might attend a twelve-step program as a sponsor and mentor with a young father. That former bishop may become one of the biggest influences for good in the young father's life.

Tip #4

Discuss the Problem, Encourage, and Avoid Shaming

PEOPLE OFTEN ASK ME WHAT they should do if they discover that a spouse, child, or quorum or ward member has a problem with pornography.

This can be heartbreaking. I have heard hundreds of rehearsed stories of spouses searching for and finding inappropriate history on the Internet. I have heard of situations where parents have walked in on children while they've been viewing pornography. I have heard the stories of bishops who have listened to heartbroken wives who had no idea their husbands were involved in it.

One of the more important steps, especially for parents, is to not shame the individual. Jesus set the perfect example: "When Jesus had lifted up himself, and saw none but the woman, he said unto her, Woman, where are those thine accusers? hath no man condemned thee? She said, No man, Lord. And Jesus said unto her, Neither do I condemn thee: go, and sin no more" (John 8:10–11).

The Savior focuses on helping this woman move forward. If individuals are going to make it through this challenge, they cannot bear the weight of constant shame. People do not improve when they feel there is nothing to fight for. For true repentance to occur, people must feel Godly sorrow. We need to allow that sorrow to happen so the Lord can work within them. Don't kick them while they're down.

At times we teach the evils of pornography without following through with the rest of the message of the Atonement and forgiveness. It is important—extremely important—that you understand that if a person discloses their actions to you, their heart has been pricked. This is not the time to shame, nor is it the time to give them a discourse about how evil the act is and how badly it will affect their future family. This is the time to help them understand the message that they can work toward sinning no more.

The reason it is so important to refrain from shaming is that pornography is often coupled with a depressive cycle. The depressed cycle goes like this: they view pornography; they feel depressed and frustrated; as the depressed feelings linger, they are drawn back to pornography because, for a few brief moments, they did not feel depressed; they view pornography again and then often feel worse.

This cycle reminds me of the verse in the scriptures where Satan "leadeth them by the neck with a flaxen cord, until he bindeth them with his strong cords forever" (2 Nephi 26:22). Pornography truly can become a "flaxen cord" and truly is "binding." Individuals who recognize this and come for help do not need to be reminded of the dangers and darkness of the path. They already know that path. They need encouragement.

Remember the great counsel we are given in Ecclesiastes: "To every thing there is a season, and a time. . . . A time to keep silence, and a time to speak" (3:1, 7). If someone comes to you showing remorse, it is time to listen and encourage. It is amazing how often in counseling I will sincerely listen and reflect someone's feelings and that person will feel very encouraged by the end of the session.

I have to be careful when I discuss human behavior so I am not misunderstood. It is rare that individuals who have been viewing pornography extensively decide one day to give it up and never return again. I hesitate to mention this because I don't want anyone to use this as a justification to go back to viewing pornography. Most often, people who work hard to overcome pornography will have setbacks, so don't get discouraged.

Even in the middle of a setback, they will need encouragement. Let me illustrate with an example. Assume I have a client who is viewing pornography multiple times a day. He really wants to change and says to his wife, "I am never going to look again." He goes three weeks without viewing any pornography, the longest he has gone for ten years, but then he gets laid off work. He feels extremely depressed; in fact, he feels like a complete failure. He heads home to find the house empty. Almost instinctively, he searches the Internet and views pornography. Two minutes into it, he catches himself and shuts off the computer. The next week in counseling, he says, "I looked at pornography again. I guess I've learned nothing, and I'm right back where I started."

I have seen this situation over and over again, and let me stress again that I share this example to in no way justify viewing pornography but to illustrate that this man *has* learned something, has begun to make changes, and is not "right back where he started." Individuals will often respond by quoting, "But unto that soul who sinneth shall the former sins return, saith the Lord your God" (Doctrine and Covenants 82:7). I have always understood this scripture to mean that our ultimate goal is to grow, improve, and change; therefore, if an individual struggling with the law of chastity continues to make mistakes, that individual is still in the process of improving. However, I personally feel that addictive behavior often will go through a cycle of improvement and setbacks until hopefully that individual has overcome a sin and will never return to it again. A man struggling to keep the law of chastity will continue to struggle as long as he continues to view pornography. If he is honestly and sincerely trying to do better and has gone three weeks without viewing but then views, he is still in the process of overcoming his struggles. He is still making progress.

May we also remember the teachings of Elder Dallin H. Oaks, "From such teachings we conclude that the Final Judgment is not just an evaluation of a sum total of good and evil acts— what we have *done*. It is an acknowledgment of the final effect of our acts and thoughts—what we have *become*. It is not enough for anyone just to go through the motions. The commandments, ordinances, and covenants of the gospel are not a list of deposits required to be made in some heavenly account. The gospel of Jesus Christ is a plan that shows us how to become what our Heavenly Father desires us to become."[10]

Elder Oaks helps us understand that change is a process. The example I gave shows individuals in a process of change, and this process will often occur in stages. This is not to justify, minimize, or excuse setbacks, but it is to help us put them in perspective.

As individuals seek to become what Heavenly Father wants, they begin to feel a sense of guilt for their actions. It is important to understand that there is a difference between shame and guilt. Guilt and Godly sorrow lead to repentance and serve as a warning, whereas shaming is destructive and does not help people improve. If they are trying to overcome pornography, they will naturally feel Godly sorrow and appropriate guilt.

Guilt is a warning signal to our souls that we have made a poor choice. It is a temporary warning to correct the choice and not return to it. In Church lessons, we often use physical examples to represent the warning system guilt provides, like how the body has a natural warning system of pain if someone touches a hot stove. If the body indefinitely felt the pain of touching a stove while it was not touching it, the body's warning system would be ineffective. If a person feels guilt when there is no need for a warning, guilt stops serving its purpose. If this continues, guilt will often lead to shame.

Shame is not a warning signal. It is a result of people feeling like there is something inherently wrong with them personally. Individuals will often use self-shame to reinforce their inappropriate beliefs that *they* are wrong, *they* are not worth anything, and *they* are defective.

If I spoke sharply to one of my children and later felt *guilty*, that feeling would lead me to apologize to my child, ask for their forgiveness, and encourage me to not do it again. Once I cleared up the problem, I wouldn't need to carry the guilt any longer. But if I said sharp remarks to one of my children and then buried myself in a bedroom and reinforced the thought that I was a terrible father, these acts would likely lead to feelings of shame. Shame does not lead to change.

Encouragement is vital when people are trying hard to break addictive cycles. When they want to continue to move away from pornography and they are trying to repent, they need encouragement because they most likely feel guilty. It is important that we help them focus on bad *choices* rather than allow them to focus on being a bad *person*.

Practical Applications

Spouses—In my own professional experience, one of the key factors in success in this changing endeavor is spousal support. Often, those viewing pornography do not want to let their companion know they have had a setback, a decision which eliminates their biggest moral support.

There is a difficult reality spouses need to know: you may have heard your spouse say something like, "I promise there is nothing wrong with you." This type of phrase often makes spouses cringe and feel more hurt, but I hope you trust me when I say that pornography is addicting and it lures people into its nasty web, but it does not mean there is a problem with you. I have seen many spouses internalize this and feel that their physical appearance is the reason their spouse views pornography. It doesn't make sense, but please trust that it is not you. Just as those struggling with pornography may be tempted to shame themselves, spouses may also be tempted to shame themselves.

Do not fall into believing that this struggle is happening because you are not beautiful enough or good enough. This is not true. If you can have the strength to focus on the problem, which is viewing pornography, and not yourself, you can become the greatest strength to your spouse.

As you spouses know, there is a level of secrecy that accompanies viewing pornography. If you can find the strength, help break down this wall. I knew a spouse who came into my office earnestly trying to help her spouse break his pornography addiction. She asked me for advice. I told her it would be extremely helpful if her husband could speak with her openly.

I told her to encourage him and let him know that she was not going to give up on him.

I watched this couple over the next few months as the husband began to share with his wife whenever he felt even the slightest bit tempted. They would talk it through without malice or blame. When the fear and secrecy were gone, this man began making huge improvements. To this day, to the best of my knowledge, this couple is thriving.

> What can you do to encourage your spouse,
> and how can you carry this out?

_____

_____

_____

Parents—This may be one of the most important things you can do for children who are struggling. I have seen young men in my office whose parents have told them they will never become a missionary, they will never be good husbands, and they will never be good priesthood holders—and the parents do this as a means to help their son "snap out of it." I plead with you not to do this.

It is important that parents develop a relationship with their children where the kids feel they can talk about these issues. I have met mothers who refuse to discuss the challenges of pornography with their sons because "that stuff is disgusting" and the mothers never thought they could "have a son like that." This attitude does not help you as a parent and certainly does not help your children.

In fact, Elder Ballard has given us great counsel on how the family and priesthood can work in conjunction. He taught:

> Too often our bishops have to instruct youth to talk to their parents about problems they are having. That procedure should actually flow the other direction. Parents should be so intimately aware of what is going on in their children's lives that they know about the problems before the bishop does. They should be *counseling with their children and going with them to their bishops* if that becomes necessary for complete repentance. As divinely appointed judges in Israel, the bishop and the stake president determine worthiness and resolve concerns on behalf of the Church; but, fathers, you have an eternal responsibility for the spiritual welfare of your children. Please assume your rightful place as counselor, adviser, and priesthood leader in preparing your sons to bear the Melchizedek Priesthood and to serve as missionaries.[11]

Parents, make sure you have discussions with your children about these topics. If a child confides in you, take this as a positive sign. They have opened lines of communication, and that takes a great deal of courage. Counsel with them, encourage them, bear testimony of the Atonement to them, and help them schedule an appointment with the bishop if needed. I am greatly encouraged when youth visit with their bishop and Mom or Dad is waiting outside to take them out to ice cream afterward. I have known many bishops who will invite the parent in to discuss the challenge together. Youth who feel love like this are more encouraged to continue. This process strengthens a youth's testimony of the love their parents have for them and the confidence their parents have in the bishop and the priesthood and emphasizes that the parent will walk through the change with them.

What time during the month can you schedule with your children to discuss important topics? (Remember that this can be formal or informal, but if you as the parent do not make it happen, it will not happen.)

Leaders—I know you are extremely busy. Having said that, I also know many of you have direct contact with specific individuals with whom you are working. Using technology for simple encouragement can go a long way. I know of a stake president who would have young men who were preparing to serve missions and were struggling with pornography text him a *V* for victory every time they resisted a temptation. The stake president would respond with a simple message of encouragement. This is a fantastic idea. You do not need to do this exact example, but setting a simple confidential way to touch base can go a long way.

> Make a list of simple ways to use technology
> to touch base with those you serve.

_____

_____

_____

_____

_____

Learn to Do Good and to Serve God with All Your Heart, Might, Mind, and Strength—Don't Just Stop Doing Evil

THE GOAL IN MAKING A change is not just to avoid evil but to do good instead. Moroni taught this principle very well: "Yea, come unto Christ, and be perfected in him, and deny yourselves of all ungodliness; *and if ye shall deny yourselves of all ungodliness, and love God with all your might, mind, and strength*, then is his grace sufficient for you, that by his grace ye may be perfect in Christ; and if by the grace of God ye are perfect in Christ, ye can in nowise deny the power of God" (Moroni 10:32; emphasis added).

Notice that Moroni mentions two major categories in which we must be engaged to come unto Christ: deny yourself of all ungodliness and love God with all your might, mind, and strength. Too often people try to overcome a pornography addiction by denying themselves of all ungodliness, or they try simply to "stop looking at pornography." I have seen this struggle too many times. They spend all of their time and energy engaged in "not looking at pornography." The problem is that making real change involves denying yourself of ungodliness *and then* spending your time loving and serving God and your fellowmen.

As human beings, we seek stimulation. No one likes to be bored or feel lazy. We constantly seek stimulation. The word *stimulation* often has a negative connotation, but stimulation describes a condition, not a specific act. For example, reading a good book can be intellectually stimulating.

When individuals stop looking at pornography, they usually notice stimulation deficiencies. First, they have more time, and second, they haven't developed productive habits to fill that extra time.

This is a common dilemma; when they stop looking at pornography, they can't find ways to fill their extra time. I often have my clients make a list of activities they can do to fill their time. If they remain bored and unproductive for long periods of time, the pull back to pornography increases.

It's exciting for me to help people discuss and develop new ways to spend their time. I love to hear them discuss things they would love to do if they were not spending so much time and energy viewing pornography. I hear things like, "Read to my children," "Go to the gym," "Do family history," "Get a certification for my career," "Coach my son's T-ball team," "Serve faithfully in my calling," "Walk the dog," "Write in my journal," "Play games with my son," "Hike with my family," "Try out for the cross-country team," "Make pinewood derby cars for Cub Scouts who do not have dads," and the list goes on.

As individuals begin to list activities they want to do, I give them three warnings. First, the activity must be engaging. An activity should make the list only if the person truly has a desire to do it and the activity is stimulating. For example, one man put fishing on his list. I asked him if he liked fishing, and he said, "It's okay if you like that kind of thing." This is the wrong kind of activity to stimulate this man.

It may not be easy to find an engaging activity, especially for those who are used to having their time consumed by secretly looking at pornography. Many people who struggle with this addiction have not engaged in positive habits in a long time, but they should stick with it until they find good, positive activities.

Second, people seeking to change habits must develop a combination of simple as well as more complex activities. They might enjoy fishing and can put this on their list, but it takes a lot of energy to load up and drive to the right fishing spot. Therefore, they will also need simple, easily accessible activities, such as playing a sports video game with their son. This is a cheap, simple activity that would allow them to spend time with their family. Find multiple stimulating activities that encourage positive habits and can be done inexpensively and, if possible, can also build stronger relationships.

Third, be cautious about filling your schedule just to fill it. Elder Dallin H. Oaks taught: "The amount of children-and-parent time absorbed in the good activities of private lessons, team sports, and other school and club activities also needs to be carefully regulated. Otherwise, children will be overscheduled, and parents will be frazzled and frustrated. Parents should act to preserve time for family prayer, family scripture study, family home evening, and the other precious togetherness and individual one-on-one time that binds a family together and fixes children's values on things of eternal worth. Parents should teach gospel priorities through what they do with their children."[12]

Remember, the goal is not to overschedule; if you're not careful, you can overschedule as a way to avoid the real problem. Sometimes people will try to fight pornography by overplanning every second of the day so as to not allow themselves or someone else to ever indulge in pornography again. This approach does not work because the real problem still exists, and once an individual has any amount of time, they are immediately drawn back to pornography.

Be careful that your list of activities is not overflowing with extracurricular activities. Look for things that will allow for more time with children or family, time for home teaching, time to watch a movie with a spouse, or time to cook a Dutch oven dinner for the kids. The goal, then, is not to overschedule but to schedule wisely.

After careful evaluation of one man's schedule who struggled with pornography, he recognized two things: first, the time of day when he was most tempted was from 5–7 p.m., after he got home from work. He also noticed that two of his sons were struggling in school. He began to spend his time from 5–6:30 p.m. with his sons, helping them with homework. One son was in elementary school, and the father had the son read to him; then he would read to his son, and they'd work on the boy's homework together. His older son would work on his homework beside them until the father was finished with the younger one, and then the father would turn his attention to him. Sometimes the father didn't understand the older son's homework, but he figured they would learn it together.

This example illustrates a few key points—this man loved his sons and wanted to see them succeed. He chose an activity that was good quality time with his family. He did not choose a new program, hobby, or time away; it was a simple activity that filled an existing need in his family. It helped him because instead of sitting on the couch, trying to resist evil by not searching the Internet, he replaced his idle time with a very positive activity.

People who are trying to break this addiction have a difficult time scheduling a "realistic" week because they are so used to filling so much time and energy either looking at or trying to access pornography. They may need additional help planning and following through with a weekly calendar, especially at first.

In the mission field, missionaries block out the week as a companionship. Even when there is a gap in time, they try to find a productive activity and place it on the calendar with an understanding that the Spirit may direct them otherwise. This could be a very helpful process for someone struggling with this addiction. Sit down and plan out a week. In the downtime, try to list effective and consistent productive activities.

The overarching principle of "do good" as opposed to "stop doing evil" is illustrated very well in the Old Testament. In the book of Nehemiah, the Jews were engaged in rebuilding their city and wall around Jerusalem. This wall served as great protection to the city and people. Opposing leaders inquired to meet with Nehemiah, and Nehemiah acknowledged that "they thought to do me mischief" (Nehemiah 6:2).

Nehemiah's response to their continued inquiries teaches a clear principle about dealing with opposition: "And I sent messengers unto them, saying, I am doing a great work, so that I cannot come down: why should the work cease, whilst I leave it, and come down to you?" (Nehemiah 6:3).

When someone is engaged in a "great work," they do not have time to look at pornography. Many individuals will say their longest period of sobriety was during their full-time mission. This provides a great insight. There can be so many reasons why this is the case, but a major factor may be that they were involved in a great work.

Practical Applications

Spouses—This is an area in which you can really help. Serve alongside your spouse. Come up with a new hobby together. I knew a couple who wanted to begin exercising together. The husband enjoyed running, and the wife enjoyed riding a bike, so she would ride ahead and then turn around and ride back to him. A simple hobby brought these two together and gave him something constructive to do instead of just avoiding doing evil.

There are so many examples of how couples can serve together, such as gardening, scrapbooking, going to the gym, or reading a book. The key is to find simple, doable activities that can bring you closer together.

Parents—I know this is a constant balancing act between not overscheduling and keeping kids from sitting around all day. It is most effective if parents are willing to sacrifice in this area. Too many times, parents want their children to find something to do because they want to be left alone to do their own thing. We all need downtime, but push yourself to find activities for you and your family to do together.

You don't need to hover over your children so they can't make any choices on their own, but help them develop the skill of "doing good" by doing it along with them. Children, especially those who have too much time on their hands with little direction, will often cause mischief. If teenagers are left to decide how they will spend their entire day, they may fill it with unhealthy activities. If children are struggling with pornography, it is important that parents help them find productive, meaningful activities where they can feel the Spirit.

One teenager who struggled with a pornography addiction began volunteering at a homeless shelter, and he felt rewarded for his service because he was making a difference in someone's life. This was a very effective way to serve God and not just avoid evil.

Leaders—We must be cautious of family time, but there are still ways we can help individuals find meaningful service opportunities, especially if they are not in a position to fully participate in all aspects of the Church. The Church welfare system is set up so bishops can help those who are receiving Church financial assistance find ways to serve. This service helps the individual feel that they are making meaningful contributions. This approach may be good for someone struggling with pornography.

If a brother discloses that he struggles every day at the same time, it might be an opportunity to have that man come with his wife to the church building to clean the chalkboards or help a widow with yard work. These kinds of activities can teach the principle of actively serving God instead of just avoiding evil.

Tip #6
Remove the Source of the Pornography

INDIVIDUALS NEED TO LEARN TO deal with sexual thoughts and triggers, but we still need to do everything we can to eliminate the source of pornography. Unwelcome thoughts may enter our minds, but we need not entertain them. Elder Jeffrey R. Holland taught:

> *Like thieves in the night, unwelcome thoughts can and do seek entrance to our minds. But we don't have to throw open the door, serve them tea and crumpets, and then tell them where the silverware is kept!* (You shouldn't be serving tea anyway.) Throw the rascals out! Replace lewd thoughts with hopeful images and joyful memories; picture the faces of those who love you and would be shattered if you let them down. More than one man has been saved from sin or stupidity by remembering the face of his mother, his wife, or his child waiting somewhere for him at home. Whatever thoughts you have, make sure they are welcome in your heart by invitation only. As an ancient poet once said, let will be your reason.[13]

The world in which we live bombards us with inappropriate material. It is a hard battle, but we must continue to fight it and avoid it however we can. Our defense mechanisms must have a two-pronged approach. The first is learning to control inappropriate thoughts. The second is that we must do all we can to remove the source of pornography.

The Savior taught, "If thy right eye offend thee, pluck it out" (Matthew 5:29). This may require altering your current habits and also making every effort to remove the source of pornography from your home and life.

Technology is constantly changing, so you will have to remain vigilant, but I have compiled a list of seven actions you can take to remove the source from your home. This is not a comprehensive list, but it will get you started.

- Make sure you have a good filter on the computer. We live in a world of pop-up ads, and it's my guess that these types of ads will become more aggressive and more targeted as time goes on. We need a good filter to block as much material as possible. There are a lot of different software companies that supply great products. Make sure whatever filter you choose can detect, identify, and block pornographic material.

    Make sure there are passwords on your Internet devices. This intervention will never be enough, but it's wise. Just about any phone, game system, computer, iPad, or iPod can access the Internet. Make sure your wireless Internet is also password protected. I stress very strongly that this will not be enough by itself to stop an addiction, but it is a wise practice. Strong passwords can really help people who are sincerely trying to overcome pornography. Viewing pornography can be a very quick reaction, and strong passwords may delay it just long enough for those being tempted to reconsider their actions. If they really want to get through the password, they can do it, but it is a helpful barrier.

- Devices should remain in open areas of the house. It is important to have computers where everyone can see what is going on. Place video game consoles in open, heavy-traffic areas. If a device is in a bedroom or office, make a rule that the door remain open and the screen face the open door.

- Be cautious of channels available through the television. I know of many individuals who began a pornography problem through basic cable and satellite channels. As time passes, more and more unacceptable material will be considered socially acceptable on basic channels.

- It may be a helpful strategy to use a recording device. Recording a show will let you skip inappropriate commercials on appropriate channels. It will also allow your family to plan your watching and avoid flipping through channels. Today, flipping through the channels is a sure way to come across inappropriate material.

- Learn how to check, record, and keep the history active on the Internet. Every parent should know how to check the Internet history, and it is also good to make a rule that no one is to clear it. There is good software that will monitor and alert family members when inappropriate sites have been accessed.

- Please be careful with what access is available in bedrooms. Any device that can get the Internet can get pornography, so if someone has a phone, iPod, iPad, video game console, Netflix, or laptop in a bedroom, they have the availability to get the Internet.

One of the new target areas for pornography markets is through video game consoles. I know many parents who have no idea what their children are doing on their consoles. We cannot remain naive and hope for the best. I have met many parents who will not allow children to watch PG-13 movies but allow them to play just about anything on a video game. We have seen through the years what has happened to the increase of inappropriate material on television. We would be naive to think that video-game marketers will not follow a similar track.

- Have everyone turn in all devices at night, even if you do not suspect there is a problem. Our culture teaches us that we must have a device at all times. It is unhealthy and many times inappropriate to be using these devices into the middle of the night. I had one mother tell me she thought her son was playing a game on the iPod and not looking at pornography. I would submit that playing a video game at 2 a.m. is not a great behavior anyway.

I hesitate to mention these seven tips because there is a chance they will be outdated within a few months. In my recent experience, portable devices are the main source of pornography. Cell phones are able to access pornography at almost anytime, anywhere, and with high levels of anonymity. I would discuss with your cell phone provider how your family's plan allows you to follow up on what content is accessed.

Practical Applications

Spouses—This is an area in which you can really help protect your family. You can, in a sense, become the guardian of the source. You can manage the passwords. You can research and manage software that will alert the family. You can think through arrangements in the home that will help put computers and devices more in the open.

Parents—Kids can often find a way around a block if they try hard enough. You will have to be vigilant. Pray for revelation for your family. Maybe it's better for your children to not have cell phones or other devices for a while. You can do this with love, and they will live through it. You can set the example of turning in devices at night. Put them in a basket and store them in your room until morning.

Leaders—Conduct a source analysis. Find out where the individuals are viewing pornography and the device they most commonly use. Help them problem solve to put themselves in a position to be successful. They may need help creating barriers to the same behavior they continue to repeat. For example, if they're looking at pornography on the iPad after their spouses go to bed, help them set up a precursor rule, like no devices or Internet after 10 p.m. Help them follow through with this rule. This will not be a cure-all, but it will help them avoid pornography while they learn to deal with the temptation.

Pornography Is Not Just a Boy Problem

Whenever I suggest that pornography is not just a boy problem, I receive some push back. Sister Julie B. Beck, former general Relief Society president, said, "Concerning spiritual wickedness, we could call attention to pornography, which is rampant. The use of pornography among our youth is growing. The new target audience for those who create pornography is young women."[14] This quote has proven true in my experience. There are times that I work with as many young women as I do young men who are struggling with pornography.

Anything that arouses the powerful sexual emotions outside of marriage that should only be expressed in marriage is inappropriate. Often, women and men are aroused differently. Men are stereotypically aroused sexually through visual and auditory means, meaning men are aroused through what they see and hear.

Stereotypically, women are more aroused through what they feel. A story line or experience is more likely to arouse them, and pornography marketers know this and seek to target these feelings.

Many prophets have warned us against the danger of reading explicit sexual material. Elder M. Russell Ballard said, "We see a rapid increase in cyberporn, involving sexual addiction over the

Internet. Some become so addicted to Internet pornography and participating in *dangerous online chat rooms* that they ignore their marriage covenants and family obligations and often put their employment at risk."[15]

Elder Oaks said the following:

> More than 30 years ago, I urged BYU students to avoid the "promotional literature of illicit sexual relations" in what they read and viewed. I gave this analogy:
>
> "*Pornographic or erotic stories and pictures are worse than filthy or polluted food.* The body has defenses to rid itself of unwholesome food. With a few fatal exceptions, bad food will only make you sick but do no permanent harm. In contrast, a person who feasts upon filthy stories or pornographic or erotic pictures and literature records them in this marvelous retrieval system we call a brain. The brain won't vomit back filth. Once recorded, it will always remain subject to recall, flashing its perverted images across your mind and drawing you away from the wholesome things in life."[16]

Both of these quotes and many others emphasize that pornography can come in more forms than visual and auditory means. I have seen this truth with young ladies and grown women who use text messaging inappropriately. There are times when young women will engage in sexual discussions with others or exchange inappropriate pictures through cell phones.

I don't share this to create paranoia but simply to break down the myth that pornography is a boy problem. The adversary is targeting women and especially young women, so we need to be aware that it is a concern.

The follow-up question is always, "What do I do?"

The first thing I would suggest is to ensure that there are no "private communications." All communication should be open among the family. A young woman should know that her mother and father can check her Facebook account whenever they want. They should know the passwords. I have met with young girls who will not even allow her parents to be "friends" on Facebook. All communication through messaging should be accessible. There is no place for erotic talk, no matter the venue.

Although pornography can start among young women through printed words, it may not remain in this form. We have young woman today who are also lured in with visual pornography. It is a growing problem, and it is no longer safe to say women are affected by pornography only if they are married to a man who views it.

Practical Applications

Spouses—Consider combining Facebook pages. Even if your accounts are separate, place pictures of your spouse, family, and children on this page. Let everyone who visits your social network account know you are married, love your family, and are not interested in inappropriate side conversations. If you begin sexual talk with a "Facebook friend," that talk will most likely turn into something inappropriate. Always be aware of your spouse's conversation history.

Parents—Consider printing out text messaging every month or so to monitor interaction. Cell phone companies will work with you in this. If your child uses a social network or e-mail, make sure you know what happens there. Teenagers usually respond by saying, "Don't you trust me?" Respond by saying, "Yes, I trust you, and I want many opportunities to validate my trust in you by observing how appropriate your interactions are."

There needs to be an understanding in the home that trust is a two-way street. If teenagers want parents to trust them, they need to demonstrate that they can be trusted. Notice in the scriptures how often sin is associated with secrecy.

Leaders—Don't assume that boys are the only ones with this challenge. Be careful not to plant seeds of curiosity, but do ask about the law of chastity. I like to read the section on sexual purity in the "For the Strength of Youth" pamphlet with young women and ask if there is anything in their life that is not in line with these descriptions. This gives a great baseline to open a discussion.

Tip #8

Learn to Develop Healthy Relationships

WE ALL WANT APPROPRIATE AND healthy relationships. As mortal beings, we have the agency to place meaning on our experiences and to train ourselves to see things as they really are.

When individuals begin to engage in pornography, they begin to disconnect with what they are *really* seeing. A therapist taught me a great technique I still use today to help a client better understand the whole picture of pornography. I will often ask a client to imagine that a camera filming pornography begins to slowly turn 180 degrees. I ask him to describe what he would see. It's difficult at first, but what happens is he begins to understand that pornography is not real. There are cameras, directors, sets, people off set prepping, and directors who yell, "Cut." There are retakes, restarts, and coaching. When someone begins to realize the nonreality of what they have been viewing, it is amazing how their desires begin to change.

There is no real connection between pornography and its user. There is no relationship. Both actors and consumers are lured carefully down to hell by the medium of an electronic device. Satan is the master deceiver. He's very good at hiding things as they really are. Individuals who have a *real* relationship are less likely to seek pornography. If they feel loved, cared for, important, and validated, the desire to view pornography for an emotional connection decreases. They also have a greater hope to succeed in breaking the addiction when they learn they have the ability to place the meaning on what they see and feel.

Elder David A. Bednar said:

> Today I raise an apostolic voice of warning about the potentially stifling, suffocating, suppressing, and constraining impact of some kinds of cyberspace interactions and experiences upon our souls. The concerns I raise are not new; they apply equally to other types of media, such as television, movies, and music. But in a cyber world, these challenges are more pervasive and intense. I plead with you to beware of the sense-dulling and spiritually destructive influence of cyberspace technologies that are used to produce high fidelity and that promote degrading and evil purposes.
>
> If the adversary cannot entice us to misuse our physical bodies, then one of his most potent tactics is to beguile you and me as embodied spirits to disconnect gradually and physically *from things as they really are.*[17]

If individuals ever disconnect pornography from what it really is, it begins to pull them into its trap. If, however, they begin to understand how to form, build, and maintain healthy relationships, they desire to have those relationships more than they desire to use pornography. It is amazing how, when a couple begins to effectively court and date again, that love increases and pornography decreases.

We all want bonding. We are drawn to each other. This is nothing to be embarrassed about or to hide. Developing a healthy relationship will help us understand what is real and what we really want.

Knowing what we want is key. We can use restaurants as a common analogy to describe the sexualized world in which we are now living. Fast-food restaurants provide food instantly, and the food is usually loaded with fat and sugar. We love this high-fat, high-sugar taste, but a short while after eating that many calories in one sitting, we begin to feel sluggish. Compare that experience to a fresh, healthy meal. Imagine fresh fruit, fresh vegetables, and slowly cooked meat with savory spices.

In my mind, there's no comparison. We all get sucked into the fast-food frenzy at times. It's easy, relatively cheap, and can even seem logical when we're pressed for time.

In this analogy, pornography would compare to fast food. Those viewing pornography do not need to court or impress the individual acting in pornography. There is no love or relationship. It is a fast-food approach to a sexual experience. However, like food that does not nourish, pornography will never satisfy or fill the need of a personal relationship. What most users really want is true intimacy and love, yet they will never realize these wonderful gifts through pornography.

We need not shy away from learning how to form true relationships. There is a growing need in the world for real relationships. Too many young people do not marry because they "do not need" the opposite sex. The adversary would have us believe that men and woman can live independent lives and achieve full happiness. Of course, there are those who will not have the opportunity in this life to marry and will be given that opportunity in the life to come, but we should never forget that marriage and intimacy has always been the standard and the program.

In learning to develop healthy sexual relationships, we need to understand that we can use our agency to assign meaning to what we see. If individuals continue to give pornography and inappropriate thoughts an erotic meaning, they will continue to struggle. If they learn that they can choose to place meaning on a thought, however, pornography begins to be much less desirable, and they begin to have more control.

For example, when people begin to understand that those producing pornography exploit human beings for profit, it begins to change the way they view that industry. They must begin to see what they are really doing.

In the book of Moses, we read about a remarkable contrast between two individuals—our glorious mother Eve and her son Cain. After Eve partook of the forbidden fruit, the Lord asked her, "What is this thing which thou hast done?" (Moses 4:19). What a humbling moment for Eve. The Lord knew exactly what she had done; He knows everything and is the greatest teacher. This was a moment when Eve had to place real meaning on what she had done. Eve responded, "The serpent beguiled me, and I did eat" (Moses 4:19).

What an example! Eve clearly stated what had happened. She was ready at that point to move forward. There is great wisdom in placing real meaning on the experience.

Compare this experience with that of Cain, who murdered his brother Abel. The Lord asked him a similar question to what He asked Eve: "What hast thou done?" (Moses 5:35). Cain's answer is insightful into a human heart that does not have any desire to change. He responded, "Satan tempted me because of my brother's flocks. And I was wroth also; for his offering thou didst accept and not mine; my punishment is greater than I can bear" (Moses 5:38). Cain did not accept responsibility, blamed someone else, and expressed concern that his punishment was too much. Cain could not accept things as they really were. I know this is an extreme example, but the Lord uses extreme examples to illustrate principles. A key principle in this story is that change requires ownership of our choices as they really are.

Individuals will often soften a pornography addiction and blame it on something else. By doing this, they are limiting their ability to make choices to change. For example, someone may describe a setback with pornography as, "I had trouble on the Internet," or "I saw some things I should not have." When I hear phrases like this, I push that person to take ownership of things as they really are. This does not mean trying to force someone to give details, but they do need to take ownership. Compare those previous vague statements to the following statement: "I intentionally sought after unclothed women who are not my wife and intentionally chose to look and be aroused." This statement describes things as they really are.

When an individual begins to take ownership of their actions, that person can see more clearly the positive movements toward a healthy relationship, and they begin to gain confidence. Consider the following description of things as they really are: "I saw an enticing picture on a magazine at the grocery store; I chose to place real meaning on that picture and not entertain the thought. I decided to think about my spouse and the goodness we have together. Exploiting women to sell magazines is a terrible practice in which I choose not to indulge." This is a great example of a person placing real meaning on a situation.

Practical Applications

Spouses—Remember to start small. Go on dates, hold hands, and stop criticizing each other. Kiss and start to develop the relationship you once had.

I would suggest doing something that sounds corny and funny to some people, but it works. I encourage couples to make a scrapbook together. Gather photos from when you met. Write memories, scan birth certificates and other important documents, add movie stub tickets from your favorite dates, and include whatever else has significance to you. This activity will help you remember and rekindle your healthy relationship. As the focus turns to strengthening the marriage relationship, your spouse will be less inclined to view pornography.

Parents—In the "For the Strength of Youth" pamphlet, it states, "When you begin dating, go in groups or on double dates. Avoid going on frequent dates with the same person. Make sure your parents meet those you date. You may want to invite your dates to activities with your family. Plan dating activities that are positive and inexpensive and that will help you get to know each other."

Encourage and teach your children how to date appropriately. I have a friend who insists on teaching his children how to date. When each boy reaches the right age, the father has his boys call their mom and practice asking her on a date. The boy has to practice telling his mom when he will be there, who else is going, when she will be home, etc. When the son picks Mom up, he opens her doors, drives cautiously, and practices talking with her. If the boy "passes," he can begin dating.

His daughters have to practice asking the right questions when he calls and asks them on a dates. She practices, "Where are we going?"; "When will we be home?"; "Who else is going?"; "When you pick me up, will you come in and meet my parents?"

Teach your children how to date. Teach them it is okay to feel nervous and uncertain and excited when they pick up their date. Help them understand that they will enjoy some dates more than others, but when they show genuine respect for another human being, they will not objectify the opposite sex. When teenagers make the connection that this boy or girl is part of a family, it makes their friendship real.

Leaders—When you are working with people who are involved with a pornography addiction, have them answer the following questions: What meaning do you choose to place on pornography? What do you truly want in a relationship in this life? What do you want in a relationship in the life to come? How must you live your life to get what you really want? What have the Lord and His prophets taught about building a healthy marriage? What has the Lord taught about healthy relationships?

This could be a great personal study for them, and they could even write it up on paper. It could be extremely beneficial for them to spend time thinking specifically about these things.

Tip #9
Do Not Look Back

IN LUKE 9:62, THE LORD TAUGHT, "No man, having put his hand to the plough, and looking back, is fit for the kingdom of God." This scripture teaches and emphasizes direction. The Lord wants us to move forward. We live in a world where many will accidently, inadvertently, indirectly, or directly come across pornography. The number of individuals in the world who have been exposed to pornography has increased significantly in the last years. A few short decades ago, an individual could "accidently" avoid pornography. That is not usually the case anymore.

Some may not agree with me when I say that this plague will not follow you forever. I have heard too many teach this topic in a way that I feel is not very edifying to those who are struggling with this addiction. I know that it does not have to continue to be a heavy daily struggle for an entire lifetime. If someone comes to the restored gospel of Jesus Christ with all of its restoration and wonder and only hears that he cannot change, that is not a saving message. I believe what the Savior declared when He said He healed those with "all manner of sickness" (Matthew 4:23).

I have a friend who always asks, "What percentage is 'all'?" It is a bold statement yet a true one. "All" is 100 percent. When the Savior says He can cure "all manner of sickness," He surely can and will include an addiction to pornography.

In an appointment one day, a woman said, "I just cannot trust him because of his pornography problem."

I noticed that her husband was visibly bothered. I asked him what was wrong, and he began to cry. This was the first time I had seen them, so I wasn't sure what to expect or if he was crying because of guilt, sorrow, or self-deprecating thoughts. He shook his head. I again asked him to explain. He looked up at me through tears and, with a level of disbelief in his voice, said, "The last time I viewed pornography was over four years ago. She knows that and still cannot forgive me."

I tried to withhold judgment until I had heard both sides. I thought maybe his wife thought he was lying. I turned to her, but she confirmed what he had said and told me she believed it had been more than four years. As I began to work with this couple, I noticed a common theme—every problem in their marriage stemmed from *his* problem. It was never her. She was dishonest in her finances and hid credit card bills from him and justified this by saying, "When I feel bad because of what he did to me, spending money makes me feel better."

I have heard and read stories of people claiming that the family pet is a higher priority than their spouse because the pet never "betrayed" them. I have met individuals who have wonderful spouses, who are wonderful providers, who sacrifice everything for their family, who have changed and left pornography, but the spouse or family has not let pornography leave them.

In these types of situations, I often think of the Lord's standard: "Wherefore, I say unto you, that ye ought to forgive one another; for he that forgiveth not his brother his trespasses standeth condemned before the Lord; for there remaineth in him the greater sin" (Doctrine and Covenants 64:9).

Please do not misunderstand me or think I am being insensitive. I have witnessed the broken homes and heartache that come from pornography. It truly is a plague that is destroying much of our society; however, I know people can change. If we do not let someone change, the greater sin remains in us.

Be careful not to use this idea as a tool of manipulation. I do not want someone who is struggling with this plague to read this section, turn to his wife, and say, "See? You have to forgive me." For those struggling with this, there are consequences for your actions, and one of those consequences may be a lack of trust from your spouse for a time.

But to those who have family members who are trying to overcome this, know that they can change. And just as the Atonement can heal someone who has been viewing pornography, the Atonement can also heal those affected by pornography viewers.

When the Lord's prophets speak about pornography, there are always two major themes: that pornography is evil and that forgiveness is possible. Sometimes in our quorums and classes, however, we are guilty of only teaching the first half of the talk. We emphasize how evil pornography is and neglect the other, essential piece.

Teaching only the evils of pornography helps no one. The person who is struggling puts his head down or leaves, and those who are not struggling make all the comments in class and often emphasize a story of someone they know who viewed pornography and ruined their family. I am not sure if anyone has benefited by the end of the lesson. Scaring people away from pornography does not work.

There *is* a place for teaching the evils of pornography because our prophets teach this principle, but the prophets and scriptures give *at least* equal, if not more, time to the principle of repentance and change.

One day, a bishop asked me to teach a lesson on pornography to his Melchezidek Priesthood holders. The bishop's invitation was unique and interesting. He said that some in the quorum would try to dominate and make statements to make others feel worse. He asked if I would ensure to cut those comments off and teach more about "how" and more about "hope."

I began teaching, and almost as if it were scripted, a man raised his hand and said, "I am single and interact with many single women. Many of them are divorced because their husbands are addicted to pornography."

I tried to follow the direction the bishop had given me to steer the conversation in a more positive direction, but inside I was really thinking about that statement. I thought, even if it was true, who was motivated by that comment? Those present who might be struggling with pornography probably just thought that divorce was the only option left for their marriages, and it didn't encourage those who were not struggling either.

It is amazing to me that we can study the scriptures and miss a major theme throughout all of the standard works: that of *change*. We can so easily accept that Alma and Paul changed. We can so easily accept that the sons of Mosiah became some of the greatest missionaries this world has ever seen. We love the stories of Alma the Elder, Lamoni, and W. W. Phelps, but so often we will not allow the man in our elders quorum to change.

Yes, it's true that images can stay in the mind. Yes, it's true that pornography is addictive. Yes, it's true that the accessibility, anonymity, and availability of pornography make it a real plague. But it is also true that people can change. I have seen it. The reason we don't usually see it is that those who have changed don't usually share it openly—and that is probably the way it should be.

Practical Applications

Spouses—Your feelings have been hurt, and it may be difficult to trust. But I know that through the Atonement of Jesus Christ, your spouse can be purified and cleansed from pornography. I have seen the devastation that comes from families who can't forgive someone who has truly repented. I know it may be difficult for you to trust again. You may want to find a support group. But please find a place in your heart to allow the one you love to change. You could be the most important support your spouse has.

Parents—Your son or daughter can have every blessing available in the kingdom of God. Many of our teenagers have buried this problem in their hearts and erroneously concluded that there is no way out. Please do not negatively fill in the blanks that have not really happened. If mothers or fathers do not believe their teens can change, why would these teens believe in themselves enough to change?

Leaders—You have keys, and I will not pretend to instruct you in this area; just know from a professional standpoint that I have seen it, and I know people can change. Knowing might serve as an added witness to strengthen your faith that individuals can overcome this. Please believe it.

Reinforce over and over Again That an Individual Can Be Forgiven

PEOPLE OFTEN ASK, "IS IT possible for someone who has indulged in pornography to change?"

I want to say one more time that I absolutely know that through the Atonement of Jesus Christ, individuals can overcome and avoid pornography.

When I hear people say they don't believe they can change or be forgiven, I feel like they do not understand the power of the Atonement. I know of men and women who are convinced that their actions are too bad and too wrong.

There are normally two false beliefs that grow out of these feelings: first, some people doubt that the Lord's Atonement can help them; second, some people doubt that they will have the strength to continue with the Lord through the healing process of His Atonement. In short, some doubt the Lord's ability, and some doubt their own ability. Occasionally, some doubt both.

Elder Scott has taught:

> I testify that when a bishop or stake president has confirmed that your repentance is sufficient, know that

your obedience has allowed the Atonement of Jesus Christ to satisfy the demands of justice for the laws you have broken. Therefore you are now free. Please believe it. To continually suffer the distressing effects of sin after adequate repentance, while not intended, is to deny the efficacy of the Savior's Atonement in your behalf.

When memory of prior mistakes encroached upon Ammon's mind, he turned his thoughts to Jesus Christ and the miracle of forgiveness. Then his suffering was replaced with joy, gratitude, and thanksgiving for the Savior's love and forgiveness. Please, go and do likewise. Do it now so that you can enjoy peace of conscience and peace of mind with all their attendant blessings.[18]

Elder Scott teaches so clearly that individuals who have fully repented and continue to suffer the effects of sin are denying the Atonement. Replace the thoughts of what you have done wrong with what the Lord has done for you. The Atonement is a miracle in the greatest essence of the word. We are allowed to change. We can change. We are encouraged to change. And we need not continually dig up old garbage.

Listen to what the Lord has said: "Come now, and let us reason together, saith the Lord: though your sins be as scarlet, they shall be as white as snow; though they be red like crimson, they shall be as wool" (Isaiah 1:18).

I love the phrase *let us reason together* in that scripture. If we imagined a conversation with the Lord in which we tried to explain to Him that we had done too much that was too wrong for too long, what would His response be? The scriptures openly teach us that our sins may be red like crimson but they can be as white as wool.

Isaiah paints an amazing picture for an object lesson. Pure wool has many strands. Each strand is so entangled with other strands that as you pull it apart, it seems like a massive, dense spiderweb. Imagine that wool being dipped in a deep, rich, dark, crimson dye. It seems from a fabric standpoint that there is no returning it to how it once was. Even if the wool were soaked in bleach, some strands would hang on to the red tint; however, when we apply the Atonement of Jesus Christ, we are not just repairing; we are becoming new creatures. We are made whole! "Behold, he who has repented of his sins, the same is forgiven, and I, the Lord, remember them no more" (Doctrine and Covenants 58:42). The Lord has promised that past sins are not remembered, nor does He want to remember them. He is omniscient, so He knows everything, but He wants us to know that He chooses to not remember repented sins anymore.

I am often asked questions about why we still remember our sins if we have fully repented. There are many reasons why remembering our sins can be a great blessing. I wish to mention only a few. First, remembering our sins serves as a great safeguard. If we had a complete memory loss of every repented situation, the odds of returning to the same exact sin would increase, and our growth would be slowed. Notice in Alma's account, he mentions that he remembered the pain no more—he didn't say that he did not remember his sin anymore (see Alma 36).

Second, we need to understand that certain precautions need to be taken to help protect the sinner and those around us. We need to understand that there is a difference between having our sins washed away and having the consequences of our sins washed away. For example, certain moral transactions may result in someone not serving in Primary or youth groups. This does not mean that the sins cannot be washed away, but it does mean that certain consequences will need to be endured during mortality. These types of consequences protect individuals.

I think of the story of the Anti-Nephi-Lehies, who covenanted never to use swords again. The Anti-Nephi-Lehies buried their weapons of war deep in the earth (see Alma 24:17). We read only a few chapters later that the people were justified in defending their families in war. So why did the Anti-Nephi-Lehies not pick up their weapons? Obviously, they had made covenants, but in my opinion, there may have been a part of this people that did not trust themselves to pick up those swords again. They had been forgiven, but they lived their lives differently as a result of their previous actions. The consequences would always stay with them and sometimes limit them, but they could still find fulfillment in life because even though the remembrance of the sin remained, they had been washed clean and could constantly draw closer to the Lord.

Please never confuse the difference between being forgiven of sin and taking precautions to protect yourself. The Lord makes it clear that you can be forgiven, but you may need to live your life differently if you have struggled with the plague of pornography. For example, I know a man who once told me that for the rest of his life, he will never use media after his wife has gone to bed. This man felt that this precaution would help in times when he knew he would be tempted most. But please do not confuse these types of examples with not being forgiven.

The principle of forgiveness is repeated throughout the scriptures. The book of Ezekiel states, "But if the wicked will turn from all his sins that he hath committed, and keep all my statutes, and do that which is lawful and right, he shall surely live, he shall not die. All his transgressions that he hath committed, they *shall not be mentioned unto him*: in his righteousness that he hath done he shall live" (18:21–22; emphasis added).

I don't know about you, but the prospect of not even having my repented sins mentioned is encouraging. We all want to change and improve. The Lord is encouraging us to recognize that when we repent of our sins, we shall live.

Doctrine and Covenants 45:3–5 gives insight into judgment. The Lord describes His role on that day. "Listen to him who is the advocate with the Father, who is pleading your cause before him—Saying: Father, behold the sufferings and death of him who did no sin, in whom thou wast well pleased; behold . . . the blood of him whom thou gavest that thyself might be glorified; Wherefore, Father, spare these my brethren that believe on my name, that they may come unto me and have everlasting life."

I imagine that on that Day of Judgment, I will not want to say much. I will not feel capable or able to defend my own case. But imagining the Savior *pleading* my cause encourages me. As a youth, my own anxieties led me to believe that the Lord was looking for reasons to keep me out of His presence. The previous passage, and others, have helped me see that Christ is doing everything in His power, while still honoring my agency, to pull me into His presence. His and His Father's work and glory is really and truly to bring to pass my and your immortality and my and your eternal life (see Moses 1:39). That is all They do—They help us succeed. They want to forgive. They want us in Their presence!

The Book of Mormon teaches, "But as oft as they repented and sought forgiveness, with real intent, they were forgiven" (Moroni 6:8). The phrase *but as oft* is so full of hope. For those struggling with any type of addiction, *but as oft* becomes a very encouraging, helpful phrase. This scripture helps us understand that we are the variable in this equation and not the Lord—the Lord will not change what He does; only we can change our actions. As often as we sincerely repent, we are forgiven.

Overcoming an addiction as well as making any kind of real change will require multiple attempts. It is encouraging and helpful to know that we are allowed and even commanded to keep trying. By giving up and not trying, we are denying the Atonement of Jesus Christ.

In the New Testament, the Lord invites us to "come unto me, all ye that labour and are heavy laden, and I will give you rest" (Matthew 11:28). The phrase *heavy laden* resonates with those with whom I have worked who have this addiction. A problem with pornography is a heavy burden to bear. There is only One who can offer true rest. He wants you to come unto Him because He is the only way out.

A Note to Those Who Struggle with Pornography

Much of this book is directed to parents, leaders, and spouses. I hope it is a valuable resource for those groups because I know that if this book were directed only to those struggling, fewer would feel comfortable carrying it around. But I now wish to address those individuals who struggle with pornography and want to change.

There are times when you feel overwhelmed, overcome, and isolated. I am sure that you feel alone at times. You might feel that you have done too much that was too wrong for too long. I have no authority or position to make a statement in behalf of anyone, but as a friend who has seen this situation many times, I ask you to believe this: I absolutely know that you can leave pornography behind. I have seen it multiple times. I have seen marriages healed, individuals rejuvenated, and families reconnected.

I have witnessed the Atonement work in powerful ways and work great miracles in individuals' lives. Many of you who are reading this now have felt the power of the Atonement in your life before. You may be at a point where you believe the Savior can help "people" but cannot help "you." I encourage you to begin where Alma encourages us to begin—if you can do no more than have a desire to believe, start there and have a desire to believe (see Alma 32). Start with a belief and a hope. You can do it. I know you can. The Lord knows you can.

I wish to state that I believe with all my heart that the Savior lives—not in an oblique way, but I believe His resurrected body is somewhere right now furthering His Father's work. I believe that He and our Father in Heaven appeared to the Prophet Joseph Smith. I know that They know your name like They knew Joseph's name. I know the Savior is the Way. It is not a question of *if* He is the answer to this problem; the question is *how* He is the answer.

I hope that these ten tips will prove helpful, and I pray that they will further discussion and exploration. I hope we can learn to control our thoughts, learn sacred sexuality, and understand when we need professional consultation. I hope we can forgive others who have harmed us and that we can forgive ourselves. Again, it is not a question of *if* the Savior is the answer; it is a question of *how* we can fully access His Atonement. And His Atonement, teachings, life, ministry, scriptures, and prophets are the way.

I know He lives and loves us, and He is *the* Way to freedom from pornography.

A Note to Suffering Spouses

You spouses are probably hurt the most through this process. I hope in some way this information is helpful. I know that throughout this book I have alluded to you being a support. This is probably the last thing you want to hear. I wanted to also mention that I know that sometimes spouses do not change and you are left to pick up the pieces. In these situations, it is even more crucial that you turn your focus to the Savior. He is the only One who can fully heal a broken heart.

Please know that in no way am I trying to neglect this crucial aspect and reality of this process. I know the Lord is the only One who can fully comprehend and help in these situations. It is tricky because I have met with spouses who needed to be more supportive, in my opinion, and I have met with spouses who were being run over by a nonchanging, uncaring spouse. Please know I am not trying to minimize any hurt. I recognize that sometimes spouses do not change.

Spouses will often ask me how long they need to endure this difficult situation. The answer to that is so personal that I do not offer my opinion. Church leaders are instructed to not counsel about when to divorce because of the personal nature of this question. I also believe that counselors need to steer clear of intimate, personal decisions such as this. These types of decisions must be made after much prayer, fasting, temple attendance, and counseling with priesthood leaders.

I do not claim that this book is a cure-all to revolutionize every pornography-inflicted marriage. The principles in this book do work when applied consistently. However, no one can control someone else's agency. The ability to choose will always be present when discussing this subject. I often think of the spouses who have endured so much and have hurt so much. I think of the scripture in the book of Revelation that states, "And God shall wipe away all tears from their eyes; and there shall be no more death, neither sorrow, nor crying, neither shall there be any more pain: for the former things are passed away" (21:4).

Helpful Reminders

1. Develop statements to replace inappropriate sexual thoughts—remember to push yourself to find real reasons for wanting to change.

2. Write about sacred sexuality—it is so important to understand that sex in and of itself is not evil. Study the scriptures and other inspired sources, and write a paper on sacred sexuality. This will help solidify your thoughts.

3. Is counseling necessary? When? Where? Who?—Remember that professional counseling is not always needed but can be helpful. Spend some time evaluating whether counseling is necessary and with whom it would be helpful.

4. Who will be the mentor to encourage daily?—Those struggling need daily contact with someone. Find a mentor who will check in and encourage you. I know this can be embarrassing, but neglecting this resource could be the difference between success and failure.

5. What are three ways the individual will build the kingdom on a weekly basis?—Remember that the point of this change is not only to refrain from evil but also to increase the amount of good.

6. What filters are being used? What other barriers are being used to eliminate the source?—Although this is not the only defense, we must make sure we have strong filters and that devices are turned in at night.

7. Do we have all access to texting, messaging, and social media?—Make it a clear expectation in the home that there are no secret conversations. Parents and spouses should be able to view e-mail, Facebook, and texting from everyone in the family.

8. Write about what the scriptures and prophets teach about healthy relationships. What will your life be like with a healthy relationship?—Writing is such a great tool. Write about what you learn from the scriptures and other sources about strengthening and forming healthy relationships.

9. What safeguards should always be maintained?—Allow yourself to change. Even those who have never struggled with pornography need safeguards in our day and age. Make rules for yourself that will help you stay far away from the line of inappropriate behavior.

10. Write a paper on what the Lord says about who He will forgive, from what, and how often—We must have rooted in our soul the belief and knowledge that the Lord can and will forgive. Studying and writing about these topics will strengthen your resolve and belief.

Endnotes

1. Jeffrey R. Holland. "Prophets in the Land Again," *Ensign*. Nov. 2006, 106–107; emphasis added.

2. Gordon B. Hinckley. "Rise Up, O Men of God," *Ensign*. Nov. 2006, 61.

3. Dallin H. Oaks. "Pornography," *Ensign*, May 2005, 89.

4. Ezra Taft Benson. *An Enemy Hath Done This* (Salt Lake City: Bookcraft, 1992), 275; emphasis added.

5. Gordon B. Hinckley. "A Tragic Evil among Us," *Ensign*. Nov. 2004, 62; emphasis added.

6. Quentin L. Cook. "Introduction to Handbook 2 and Related Principles," Worldwide Leadership Training, 2010.

7. Jeffrey R. Holland. "Personal Purity," *Ensign*. Nov. 1998; emphasis added.

8. Gordon B. Hinckley, "A Tragic Evil among Us," *Ensign*. Nov. 2004, 62.

9. List adapted from the *DSM-IV-TR*, 202.

10. Dallin H. Oaks. "The Challenge to Become," *Ensign*. Nov. 2000, 32.

11. M. Russell Ballard. "The Greatest Generation of Missionaries," *Ensign*. Nov. 2002, 48; emphasis added.

12. Dallin H. Oaks. "Good, Better, Best," *Ensign*. Nov. 2007, 105.

13. Jeffrey R. Holland. "Place No More for the Enemy of My Soul," *Ensign*. May 2010, 45; emphasis added.

14. Julie Beck. "Teaching the Doctrine of the Family," Seminaries and Institutes of Religion Satellite Broadcast. August 2009.

15. M. Russell Ballard. "Let Our Voices Be Heard," *Ensign*. Nov. 2003, 18; emphasis added.

16. Dallin H. Oaks. "Pornography," *Ensign*. May 2005, 88.

17. David A. Bednar. "Things as They Really Are," CES Fireside for Young Adults. May 3, 2009.

18. Richard G. Scott. "Peace of Conscience and Peace of Mind," *Ensign*. Nov. 2004, 18.

Author Bio

G. SHELDON MARTIN IS A seminary teacher and a clinical mental health counselor. He grew up in Palmdale, California; attended Ricks College and BYU; and served a mission to Paris, France. He is a favorite speaker at Education Week, EFY, Best of EFY, and at youth conferences around the country. With a master's degree in mental health counseling, he specializes in the areas of pornography addiction, parenting, marriage, anxiety, depression, and struggling teens. Sheldon is completing his postgraduate doctoral degree at Arizona State University in Behavioral Health. He and his wife, Nicole, are the parents of five children. He is currently serving as bishop of his ward.